WHAT IS A FLOWER?

What is a
FLOWER?

by Jenifer W. Day

illustrated by Dorothea Barlowe

gb GOLDEN PRESS • NEW YORK
Western Publishing Company, Inc., Racine, Wisconsin

TABLE OF CONTENTS

This is a daylily.
A daylily is a wild flower
    with large, fragrant blossoms.
Its flowers form seeds
    to grow new plants.

There are many kinds
    of wild flowers.

Columbine

Dandelion

Poppy

Daisy

Violet

This is a carrot.
A carrot is a garden vegetable.
Its flowers form seeds
    to grow new plants.

There are many garden
    vegetables with flowers.

Cauliflower

Peas

Artichoke

Squash

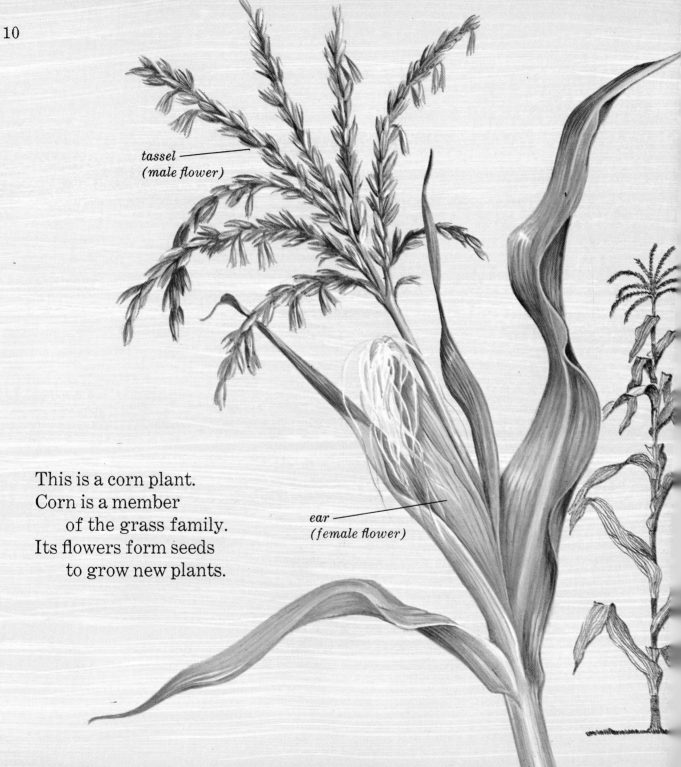

tassel
(male flower)

ear
(female flower)

This is a corn plant.
Corn is a member
  of the grass family.
Its flowers form seeds
  to grow new plants.

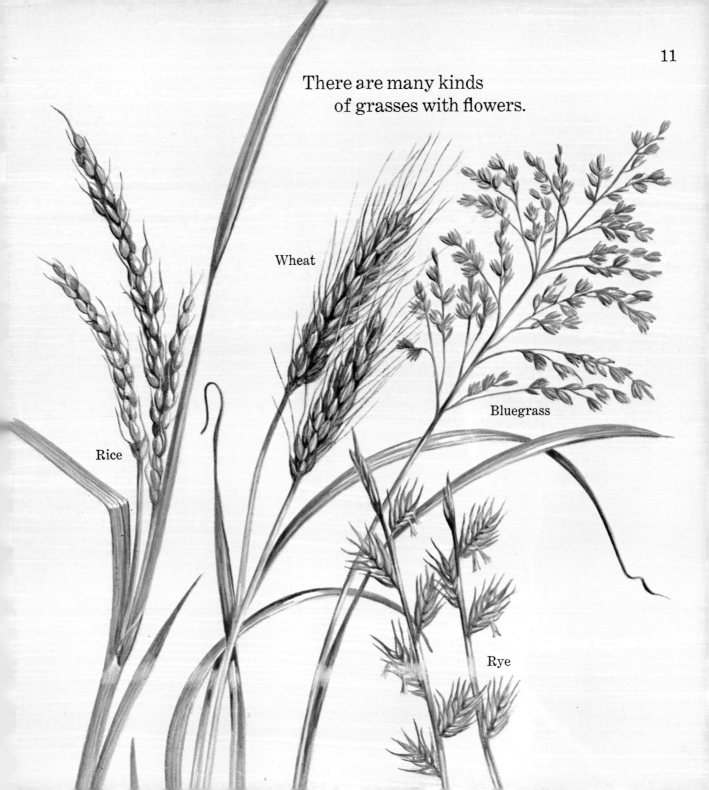

There are many kinds
of grasses with flowers.

Wheat

Bluegrass

Rice

Rye

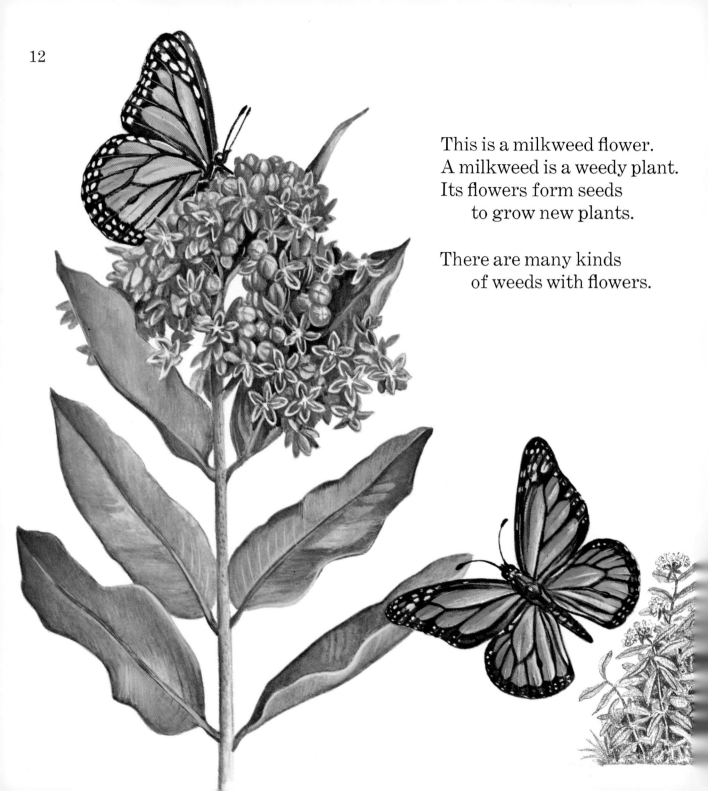

This is a milkweed flower.
A milkweed is a weedy plant.
Its flowers form seeds
      to grow new plants.

There are many kinds
      of weeds with flowers.

Goldenrod

Chicory

Cudweed

Lady's Thumb

This is a flower
    from a yellow-poplar.
A yellow-poplar is a tree.
It is sometimes called
    a tulip tree.
Its greenish flowers are
    shaped like tulips.
Its flowers form seeds
    to grow new plants.

There are many kinds
    of trees with flowers.

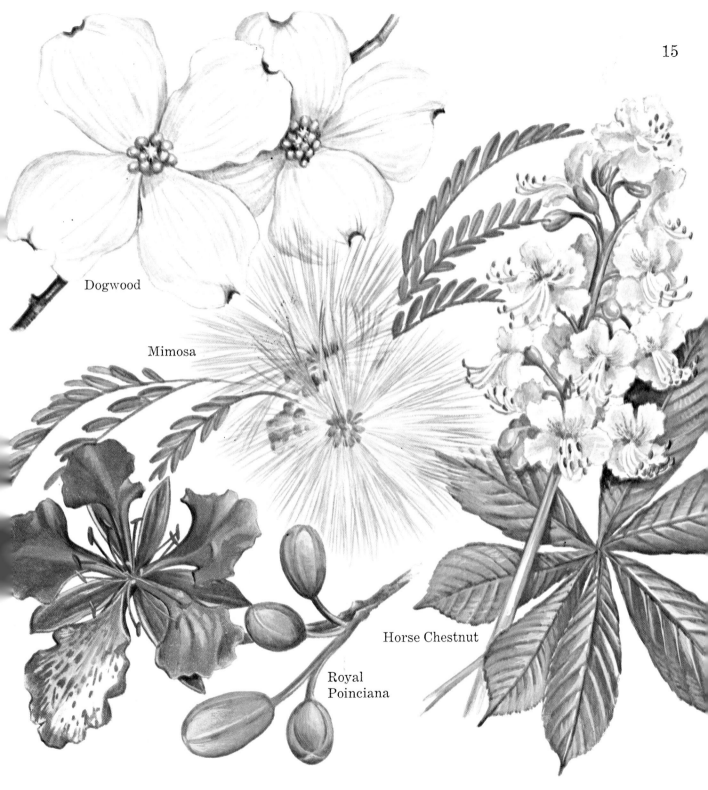

Dogwood

Mimosa

Royal
Poinciana

Horse Chestnut

This is a rhododendron flower.
A rhododendron is a shrub
    that has evergreen leaves.
Some rhododendrons
    have white flowers.
The flowers form seeds
    to grow new plants.

There are many kinds
    of shrubs with flowers.

Hibiscus

Lilac

Swamp
Azalea

Forsythia

This is a rose.
A rose is a thorny plant
    that is grown mainly
        for its beautiful flowers.
Some members of the rose family
    are grown for their fruits.

The fruits come from the flowers
    and the seeds are in the fruit.

Hawthorn

Plum

Apple

Black Cherry

There are many members in the rose family.

This is a trumpet vine.
Its stems twine around fence posts,
    along fences, around other plants,
    or climb on any support that is handy.
Its flowers form seeds
    to grow new plants.

There are many kinds
    of vines with flowers.

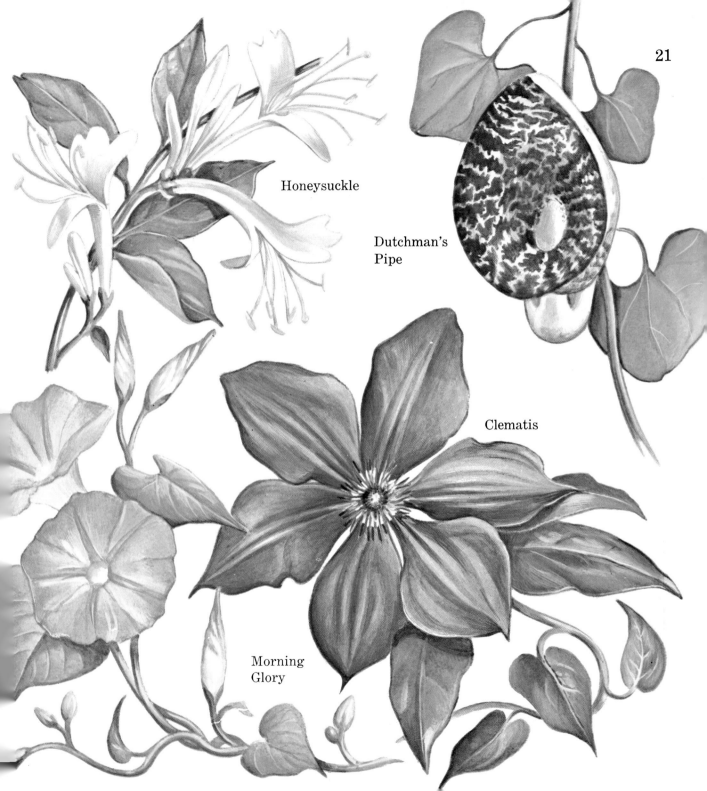

Honeysuckle

Dutchman's
Pipe

Clematis

Morning
Glory

This is an orchid.
An orchid is an exotic plant that
    usually grows in the tropics.
The flowers form seeds
    to grow new plants.

There are many
    exotic plants with flowers.

Bird-of-Paradise

Night-blooming
Cereus

Yucca

Bromeliad

This is an iris lily.
An iris is a garden flower.
Iris flowers form seeds
    to grow new plants.
But most irises are
    grown from bulbs.

There are many kinds
    of garden flowers.

Zinnia

Hollyhock

Tulip

Pansy

This is a pitcher plant.
Pitcher plants are carnivorous.
They feed on insects.
Their flowers form seeds
    to grow new plants.

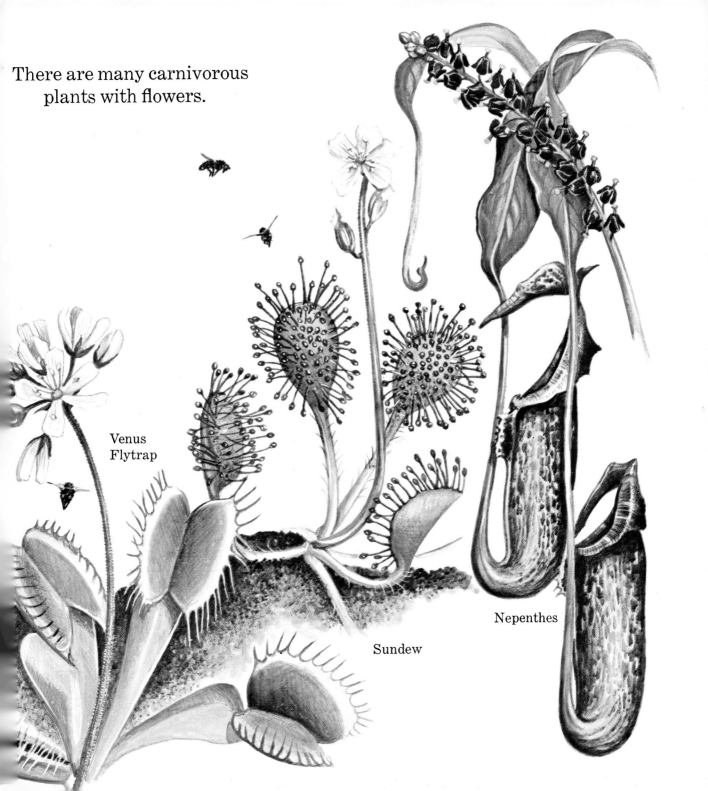

There are many carnivorous plants with flowers.

Venus
Flytrap

Sundew

Nepenthes

There are many kinds
    of plants with flowers.
Weeds have flowers.
Vines have flowers.
Trees and shrubs have flowers.
Vegetables have flowers.
    and grasses have flowers.
Even flowers have flowers.
The flowers may be big
    and showy.
Or they may be very small
    and hardly
    show at all.
Flowers come in many colors,
    and every flower
    has a job to do.

But, what is a flower?

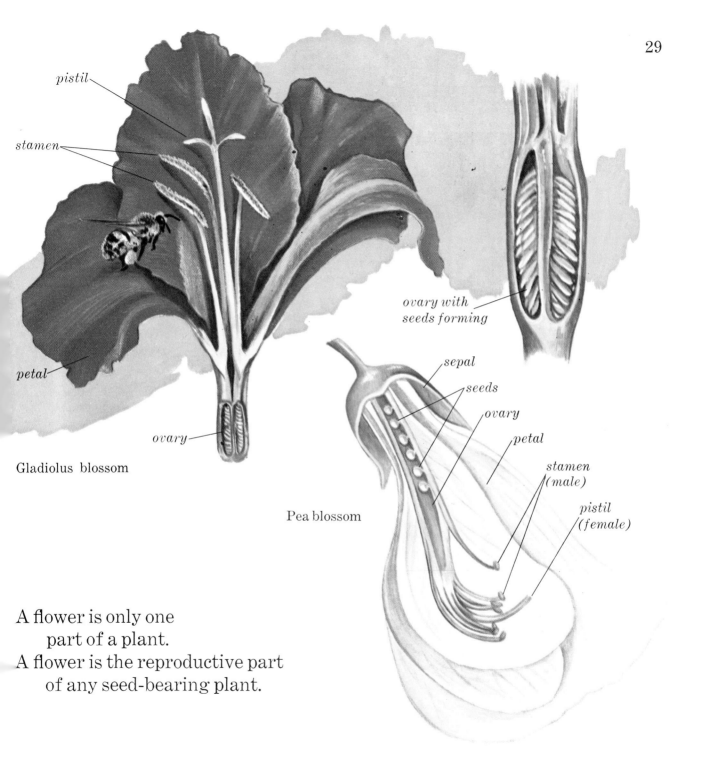

pistil

stamen

petal

ovary

Gladiolus blossom

*ovary with
seeds forming*

sepal

seeds

ovary

petal

*stamen
(male)*

*pistil
(female)*

Pea blossom

A flower is only one
    part of a plant.
A flower is the reproductive part
    of any seed-bearing plant.

WORD LIST

WORDS THAT NAME

blossom(s)	grass(es)	pistil	support
bulb(s)	insects	plant(s)	tassel
carrot	iris	post(s)	this
corn	lily	rhododendron	tree
daylily	member(s)	rose	tropics
family	milkweed	seeds	tulip(s)
fence(s)	orchid	sepal	vegetable(s)
flower(s)	ovary	shrub(s)	vine(s)
fruit(s)	part	stamen	weed(s)
garden	petal	stem(s)	yellow-poplar

WORDS THAT DESCRIBE

any	grass	new	some
big	greenish	pitcher	thorny
beautiful	handy	reproductive	trumpet
carnivorous	kinds	rose	weedy
exotic	large	seed-bearing	white
fragrant	like	showy	wild
garden	many	small	yellow

ACTION WORDS

are	come	grow(s)	is
called	feed	grown	shaped
climb	form	have	twine

NOTE TO PARENTS AND TEACHERS

Children today are faced with a knowledge explosion unprecedented in recorded time. It is forcing parents, educators, and publishers to reexamine the kinds of books we place at their disposal. We must take shortcuts to expedite and expand their level of understanding. For that reason, this book, which is one of a series, has been designed as a beginner's introduction to concept development.

Flowering plants, the most recently evolved and the most dominant plants in existence today, number about 250,000 species. They include the woody plants—trees, shrubs, and vines, but the majority are herbaceous. This book introduces, in a very elementary way, the notion of how these plants are classified by using a representative sampling of different groups of flowering plants. Each species illustrated is identified by its common name. At the same time the differences among species are being displayed, there is a continuity developed through a repetition of those characteristics held in common by all flowering plants. The flower structure is identified as being the reproductive part of seed-bearing plants, no matter how different one species is from another. This simple introduction to flowering plants may initiate an early awareness of their importance to the continuity and maintenance of life.

While there has been no attempt to restrict the vocabulary to conform to standard readability levels, there has been an attempt to repeat words often enough to develop word recognition, even among the very young. It is supposed that this book may be used with children who are, as yet, non-readers. It is the philosophy of the author that many children suffer from mental retardation engendered by an all too common malady—lack of exposure. For that reason, there has been a deliberate introduction of words not usually found in books for this age level, but only those words needed to convey the concepts of diversity and uniformity among living things. It is to be assumed that any word that is understood orally may be learned visually, especially if it is encountered often enough to make an indelible impression.

The word list found on pages 30-31 has been included for those of you who wish to help some child practice word recognition out of context. The words have been divided into three groups according to the way they have been used in the text. Not all words used have been listed. At no time is it suggested that the use of the word list be extended beyond the child's own interest in learning the words included. It is simply an optional memory exercise.

432
$ 7.50

DATE DUE

MAY 3 '93			